THANK
YOU
FOR TALKING
ABOUT ME!

Lies, Slander, Envy, Accusations and Deceit:
The New Attack of An Old Enemy

BILL ADKINS

TATE PUBLISHING, LLC

Published in the United States of America
by Tate Publishing, LLC
127 East Trade Center Terrace
Mustang, OK 73064
(888) 361-9473

Scripture quotations marked "KJV" are taken from the Holy Bible, King
James Version, Cambridge, 1769.

ISBN: 1-933148-56-X

TABLE OF CONTENTS

FOREWORD

Generally, words of gratitude are expressed after a positive deed is done for an appreciative recipient. "Thank you" are two small words totaling eight letters that articulate an emotion felt for someone else's kindness. These statements are the norm, however in the case of this book's title, it is so much the reverse that it appears to be all-encompassing the abject opposite of words that assemble for a positive expression of congeniality.

"Thank You For Talking About Me" is more the intangible and spiritual view in how negative expressions are used for good in the realm of God and God's purpose in our lives. How dare one thank another for "talking about him or her." We jump towards the opportunity to thank friends, family, or in some instances complete strangers, for a kind word, expression of favor, or even a light-hearted compliment. In my husband's book, he means it! Each time he hears negativity about himself personally; his past life; or his ministry, he blesses God. He wants to shout hallelujah and thank the weak, unsaved, or unknowing for conveying a bit of malevolence against him. For it is in that vote of non-confidence, berating, jealousy, envy, or just down-right ungodliness that he knows he will receive the blessing and gain even more the favor in the eyes of He whom he serves so diligently and consistently.

There have been times in our lives when the surprise comes from what many would call "the most unlikely source." He will hear that he has been talked about by one of his dearest friends, or by one of his own members, or by a valued employee, or board member whom he has so enthusiastically promoted and appointed. At these times he hurts, naturally, not unlike we all have as school students when we hear of what those whom we hold in high-esteem thinks about us.

I believe that we are all that same 6th grader or 10th grader. It hurts to hear that others do not feel about us as we do about them. But with his hope in the Lord this apostle remains unwavered and undeterred.

-Mrs. Linda Kerr Adkins

A BRIEF INTRODUCTION

"Bless them which persecute you: bless,
and curse not." Romans 12:14

I would like to begin this book with a touch of sarcasm and acrimony by offering my sincerest thanks to all those who talked about me. I want to especially thank all those who lied on me. I would like to show my gratitude and appreciation for all those who persecuted me. To those who gossiped about me, I want to offer you my thanks. To those who sought to harm me, I want to thank you, as well. To all those who said I wouldn't make it, my sincere and warmest regards. To all my jealous brothers and sisters in ministry who maligned and chastised this ministry, I thank you from the bottom of my heart. For everyone of you that said Adkins is radical, God bless you. To all of you who said Adkins is too controversial, thank you so much. To all of you who said Greater Imani Church and Christian Center would never grow, thank you, thank you, thank you!

And before I conclude, I want to give a shout-out to the devil and thank him for inspiring me as well. What he meant for evil, God meant it for good.

Chapter One

JEALOUSLY IN GOD'S COUNTRY

*"And I say also unto thee, That thou art Peter, and
upon this rock I will build my church; and the gates of
hell shall not prevail against it." Matthew 16:18*

There are times when the gates of hell seem to swing from inside out. There is a new attack of an old enemy and the Lord's church is still the target. The tactic is to destroy the church from within, utilizing frustrations in ministry, undetached goals and mercurial expectations of some who may have misjudged their anointing and calling.

Addressing a national seminar of Southern Baptist leaders, George Gallup (the pollster) said, "We find there is very little difference in ethical behavior between churchgoers and those who are not active religiously . . . the levels of lying, cheating, and stealing are remarkably similar in both groups. Gallop said, "Eight out of ten Americans consider themselves Christians, yet only about half of them could identify the person who gave the Sermon on the Mount, and fewer still could recall five of the Ten Commandments. Only two in ten said they would be willing to suffer for their faith."

Jealously in God's country is not new, but contempt and anger towards other ministries, with veracity is. Paul writes to the church at Ephesus in 6:11:

" . . . *Stand against the wiles of the devil."*

The word "wiles" in the Greek means "methodical." The Lord wants us to investigate those methods and settled plans, crafty tricks, and schemes that the enemy uses against us.

The Lord Jesus led me to organize Greater Imani Church and Christian Center on the morning of November 1, 1989. I had been serving as the pastor of a small Baptist church in north Shelby County, Tennessee for four years. Little John Missionary Baptist Church was my first pastorate. Quickly, I realized the frustrations that many "elected" pastors must feel; the coming to a congregation which does not want to grow, develop, mission, or even disciple. The enthusiasm and passion of a young preacher is overpowering and compelling. The zeal to "go ye therefore" drives the images of great services, ministries, and accomplishments for the Lord. But reality teaches that there are those in the church who do not want to go anywhere other than to Sunday worship service.

The Lord Jesus called me while I was working as a talk show host for a local radio station. I had been in the media spotlight for twenty-four years as a disc jockey, newsperson, TV news anchor, and talk show host. My name was already "household" in the Memphis community and my face appeared on television commercials and billboards. My ratings in radio confirmed a successful and popular career. When the Lord called me to ministry I came equipped with those media skills that would prove paramount. Everything in the past is intended to help accomplish things in the present. God weaves us into His fabric according to His own pattern for us. Our backgrounds are not coincidental nor happenstance. Everything good and bad in our past helps to accomplish the purpose of God in and through us.

> *"But by the grace of God I am what I am: and his grace which was bestowed upon me was not in vain; but I laboured more abundantly than they all: yet not I, but the grace of God which was with me."*

> *1 Corinthians 15:10*

The Lord released me from that pastorate and I began to seek after His purpose for me. With the vision of the new ministry came the blueprint of how it was to be accomplished. The Lord not only gave me the vision but He also gave me the plan. I could see clearly this great ministry developing over a period of twenty-one years (at the time of publishing we are beginning our fifteenth year). I began with twenty-nine family members and friends assembled in my home. The second week almost forty gathered and by the third week we knew we had to move. The Lord, through my friend in radio and now one of my deacons, James Chambers, led us to an unfinished sanctuary in the

Frayser Community of Memphis, Tennessee. The church that had begun construction voted to move to another location and abandon the project, settling for a financial loss. We entered that building with no heat, plumbing, or electricity and within three months our membership had grown to over four hundred. Within six months, we had eclipsed six hundred.

I utilized all my media skills, establishing radio programs, a television ministry, and aggressively discipling the unchurched and unsaved. We moved to a larger facility, purchased another, and then another. In the course of seven years the ministry had topped six thousand members and was one of the most visible and active ministries in Memphis and the Mid South. The ministry had established and/or supported three medical missions in West Africa (Senegal, Gambia, & Ghana). The Imani Telecast Network USA was founded and the weekly broadcast was seen in over twenty million homes. (At time of publication our television audience has grown to over 48 million homes.) God's favor was displayed upon us in all pure excellence. Our obedience was the key and our energy and enthusiasm was our launching platform. We were, and still are, youthful, exuberant, but humble.

If we are truly humble we shall in a little time know the advantages of God's favor; He will lift us up out of trouble; He will lift us up in our spirits and comfort us under trouble; He will lift us up to honor and safety in the world; or He will lift us up on our way to heaven, so as to raise our hearts and affections above the world.

"God will revive the spirit of the humble."

Isaiah 57:15

"He will hear the desire of the humble."

Psalm 10:17

God will lift the humble up to glory. Before honor is humility. The highest honor in heaven will be the reward of the greatest humility on earth.

Humility is, first of all, the recognition that everything we are and everything we have is a gift of God's grace. If we have a talent - it is because He has given it to us. If we are wise - it is because He has made us so. If we have a particular spiritual gift, it came from His Spirit. If we are rich, He enabled us to earn the money. We cannot take credit for anything; all glory must go to God. We should reflect this attitude in "lowliness of mind." You see, it is possible to be "too big" for God to use you but never "too small" for God to use you!

While we were humble, others within the community of faith were outraged. Who do they think they are? Where did they come from? Are they based in bible truth or are they merely a gimmick or a "new fad or buzz church?" And what about their pastor, is he truly a preacher or is he still a public speaker? These were the questions permeating the Memphis religious community.

I, and my ministry, came under attack. This attack came from within the body and because of that, it hurt deeply. My wife and children also learned the realities of jealously in God's country. My children could not just be children, they were "my children" and they heard the reverberated words of malice that came through parents. Linda, my wife, quickly had to adjust to the flow of lies and slander that seemed to change weekly as to just how this ministry became so successful so quickly. There were personal confrontations in public places. I remember one minister accosting us saying, "You must not be teaching the Word because churches just don't grow that fast." I asked him if the first six chapters of Acts were missing from his bible. Harsh words deeply rooted in envy attacked the membership. Bitter and poorly chosen words spoken from pulpits were echoed by members. False accusations and lies, became commonplace in a community of faith which supposedly lifted Jesus Christ as its ensign and Master.

Our tears sometimes flowed like rivers. I remember a warning issued to me by Bishop G. E. Patterson, Presiding Bishop and Chief Apostle of the Church of God in Christ. At a gathering of ministers at his church, Bountiful Blessings, that I helped coordinate the Bishop publicly said, "It is good that Bill Adkins could bring us together, but when "Little John" becomes "Big John" you'll see a difference in how the brothers will treat you." The Bishop's words were prophetic, but the growth did not come at Little John Missionary Baptist Church, it came at Greater Imani Church and Christian Center, same difference!

I soon realized just how immense was the frustration of so many that desired to serve God in excellence. Traditional churches and pastors were all trapped by their own method and process. They could not grow and would not adapt to a changing landscape. This is the frustration that becomes the fertile ground for the entrance of the enemy.

There is a "new move" of Christ in the earth. New churches with the same gospel message, but heightened and lifted with new mentalities and convictions are marching forth with the battle cry of salvation and discipleship in end-times ministry. These churches are most often non-denominational and that, too, causes division and distrust.

The core element of these attacks is fear, coupled with envy. God says it's time for a "new thing" in the earth. Traditional ministries with traditional pastors and traditional concepts may be afraid of what God is doing now. This fear must be confronted with faith and reason. One pastor asked me, "Why can't we all just stay the same. Why do I need to learn something else?" With the answer being obvious I shared with him that he need not fear what God was doing, but rejoice in it. Fear imprisons, faith liberates; fear paralyzes, faith empowers; fear disheartens, faith encourages; fear sickens, faith heals; fear makes useless, faith makes serviceable and, most of all, fear puts hopelessness at the heart of life, while faith rejoices in God.

Chapter Two

LEARNING TO LOVE THE UNLOVELY

"But I say to you, love your enemies and pray for those who persecute you."

Matthew 5:44 (RSV)

Clarence Darrow, the famed criminal lawyer, once joked: "Everyone is a potential murderer. I have not killed anyone, but I frequently get satisfaction out of obituary notices."

This is the toughest lesson to learn. Loving our enemies is almost unthinkable for some of us. Some see the necessity to fight our enemies, and to give them back evil for evil. Some want to hurt those they know have hurt them. One of the failings of humankind is anger. We are too quick to foster anger against those who come against us. It is our human frailty that makes us think others can hurt and harm us, but in fact they only improve us.

"Recompense to no man evil for evil. Provide things honest in the sight of all men. If it be possible, as much as lieth in you, live peaceably with all men. Dearly beloved, avenge not yourselves, but rather give place unto wrath: for it is written, Vengeance is mine; I will repay, saith the Lord. Therefore if thine enemy hunger, feed him; if he thirst, give him drink: for in so doing thou shalt heap coals of fire on his head. Be not overcome of evil, but overcome evil with good."

Romans 12: 17—21

When you think about it, every bad thing that has happened in our lives became a "turning-point" for our ultimate deliverance. I will go even further and say that the best things that happened in our lives only happened after some form of attack by the enemy. Let's take this a step further; I am suggesting that whatever you are now, wherever you are now in your relationship with the Lord, is directly related to how much you have suffered at the hands of the enemy.

Here's a thought: Where would you be without an enemy?

There is a heavenly scheme that must be discerned and detected, a scenario of life that must be played out to the fullest. We must live and suffer until we understand the purpose of suffering. We must endure until we see the picture clearly. The plot will thicken, but understanding will come. Here is part of that understanding:

Your enemies sometimes render you favors that your friends cannot deliver!

We love to say, "If it had not been for the Lord by my side, where would I be?" But let's ask the question, "If it had not been for our enemies, where would we be?" This may be a radical consideration, but consider it please. Without the provocation of the enemy, most of what we have accomplished would not have been accomplished. It is the love and mercy of God that strengthens us but it is the evil and contempt of the enemy which provokes us.

It was your enemy, not your friend who moved you closer to the Lord. It was your enemy, not your friend, who brought you down on your knees. It was your enemy, not your friend who made you cry out the name of Jesus. It was your enemy, not your friend who made tears of consecration fall from your eyes. It was the action of your enemy who made you realize your humility before a mighty God. It was your enemy who delivered you to the ground of God's mercy.

It is the course of God's people, in this world, to be persecuted by the men of it, in some shape or another, either by words or deeds. To have a mouth full of anger, cursing and bitterness is the character of an unregenerate man. This by no means suits one who names the name of Christ for blessings, and then has cursing proceed out of the same mouth. It's hard to love unlovely people, but we are commanded to love those who persecute us. There is before us a great door of blessings and opportunity,

19

but there are many adversaries. It is our adversaries that attempt to block us from those blessings and opportunities, but if we are wrapped in the blood of Christ, they effectually will assist us in reaching our goals. With knowledge of their methodical attempts to hurt us, we embellish our relationship with God by learning to love them.

> *"So shall they fear the name of the LORD from the west, and his glory from the rising of the sun. When the enemy shall come in like a flood, the Spirit of the LORD shall lift up a standard against him."*
>
> *Isaiah 59:19*

There is a standard, a rod of God that will rise in defense of you. Your enemy will always think he has the victory, but the ultimate victory is always truly ours.

People will always come against you. There are those that live only to lie about you. There are those whose only desire is to hurt you.

> *The Lord is not slow in keeping his promise, as some understand slowness. He is patient with you, **NOT WANTING ANYONE TO PERISH,** but everyone to come to repentance."*
>
> *2 Peter 3: 9 (NIV)*

Our desire is to see our enemies defeated and damned, but the Lord's desire is to see them come to

***repentance. Your hurt by them is possibly God's plan
for their deliverance.***

The writer of Proverbs wrote in chapter 24 verses 17–18,
*"Do not gloat when your enemy falls; when he stumbles, do not
let your heart rejoice, or the LORD will see and disapprove and
turn his wrath away from him."* I want to thank my enemies for
all the evil they have caused in my life. I want to thank every
person who lied about me. I want to thank every person who
perpetrated a plot against me. I want to thank every evil-doer
for every scheme, plot, ploy and evil device utilized against me.
I want to thank every person who denied me an opportunity. I
want to thank every person who owed me money and did not
pay me back. I want to thank every person who doubted me. I
want to thank every person who troubled me. I want to thank
every person who ever cursed me.

I realize that there is a plan above the plan. We must
go deeper in our quest to see God's salvation and deliverance.
Everything that looks bad is not. Sometimes deliverance comes
disguised as trouble. Therefore we must patiently wait for God
to reveal the purpose what appears to be persecution.

Love the unlovely!

Chapter Three

DEALING WITH GRASSHOPPERS

And they brought up an evil report of the land which they had searched unto the children of Israel, saying, the land, through which we have gone to search it, is a land that eateth up the inhabitants thereof; and all the people that we saw in it are men of a great stature. And there we saw the giants, the sons of Anak, which come of the giants; and we were in our own sight as grasshoppers, and so we were in their sight.

Numbers 13:32,33

The enemy of God uses discouragement and doubt as his main weapons against grasshoppers. He does not have to attack with inclinations of evil; all he has to do is to seed doubt against the backdrop of God's intended blessings. Grasshoppers cannot face their own personal fear but are willing to lie to protect their image. These are faithless persons within the body that would rather be jealous than believe God for their own victory.

Satan causes the people of God to distrust God, His power and promise, thereby counseling them to rely upon their own rationales. God promised Moses a land flowing with milk and honey. Even the spies that went in to scout the land could not deny that it was indeed, a land rich and fruitful. Thus, even out of the mouth of adversaries, God will still be glorified and the truth of his promise attested. Just like some of us today, we want rain without thunder, sunshine without heat, coldness without ice and prosperity without work.

True believers know that God delivers and He does not lie. God sets it out or sets it in motion. It is the movement of faith that delivers.

"For as the body without the spirit is dead, so faith without works is dead also."

James 2:26

These so-called believers and rumor-mongers were unwilling to regard God's promise as final. They saw a people bigger than they were. So they reduced themselves, in their own minds, to grasshoppers. They qualified themselves as insects in what could have been an exercise of faith against the enemy of God.

It's a shame that the devil can win so many battles without so much as even a fight. But people who have not manifested the Word of God into their very fiber are not ready to do battle with the enemy. Superficial Christianity is the calling card of an unbeliever. Instead of worshiping God, these people worship "church." They've grown up in church but they haven't grown up in God. They have acquired all the motions and rituals of faith, but don't actually believe nor trust God's provision for them. These spies deserved to be branded as cowards, but the scripture branded them as unbelievers.

> ### *People who grow up in church do not necessarily grow up in the Lord!*

They came to Canaan with human probability instead of spiritual possibility. They had the manifest and sensible tokens of God's presence with them, and the engagement of his power with them. Time and time again, God showed Israel that no nation or force was more powerful than they, as long as God was with them, yet they could not move in faith.

People come to church looking for God but "church" gets in the way. "Church people" will accommodate themselves with the conveniences of comfort. They will choose to stay where they are and design or develop rules and even bylaws that further stipulate this intention. Meanwhile, they develop disdain for those who move on spiritual possibility. Instead of making war against the common enemy of the faith, they choose to make war against the body. Larry Crab, in his book "Soul Talk," writes, "The theology of religion can be expressed in a simple tenet: The effort to harness whatever power is available in the service of whatever goal we value is a right and noble endeavor."[1] For many traditional churches, religion has become the object of adoration, and not the Lord Jesus Christ. Grasshoppers have to lie and distort. Their faith is weak but their religion is mighty. The politics of church, denominations, and fellowships nurture a paranoia of God's "new move."

"Wherefore, my beloved, as ye have always obeyed, not as in my presence only, but now much more in my absence, work out your own salvation with fear and trembling. For it is God which worketh in you both to will and to do of his good pleasure. "

Philippians 2:12,13

Ancient Israel's problem was that they thought their power was in their rituals and traditions, rather than in God. When Jesus came to the earth, numerous Jewish scholars refused to believe that He was the Messiah, because He did not come according to their rituals, traditions, and prophecies. There are many people today whose problem is that they prefer ritual and tradition over function and presence.

Millions of people from every Christian denomination fit this same sad description. Many trust in church membership to get them to heaven, while others trust in religious traditions. Some believe they will make it to heaven because they are "good" people; they try to do the right thing, at least most of the time. Even though they attempt to do good, and even though they attend worship service regularly, they are lost in church.

St. Augustine prayed, "Thou has made us, O Lord, for Thyself, and our souls are restless until they find their rest in Thee." The objective of every true believer and worshipper is to find rest in the Lord. Being in attendance at a worship service is not truly worshipping the Lord.

Rest in the Lord cannot be found through attacks on the body. The unbridled mouth becomes the voice of fear and frustration. The notion is to verbally attack anything that is different, especially progressive and successful. This kind of religious bigotry and arrogance grows out of fear.

I have a unique background. I was educated in Catholic Schools, worshipped in a Disciples of Christ Church, then a Baptist Church, and mentored by an agnostic Football Coach. These four varying influences tossed me to and fro, confusing an already confused teenager even more. I clearly remember that I did not like religion. I perceived religion as divisive and argumentative. Everyone I knew argued about it. I was warned by my mother never to discuss it. I can remember church fights that ended up in courts. Preachers pointing pistols at deacons and deacons changing the locks on sanctuary doors were commonplace. I remember Church of God in Christ folks saying Baptist folks were not saved. I remember Baptist folks saying anyone not immersed in water was not truly baptized. I remember Methodists saying "It doesn't take all that!"

The enemy seeks to define territories for us that will keep us embattled against one another. Most of the people who talked about me knew very little of me. They formulated opinions based on other people's opinions that were based on, guess what, other people's opinions. They never had a clear thought of their own regarding this "renegade" preacher and his new congregation.

> *"There is that speaketh like the piercings of a sword: but the tongue of the wise is health."*
>
> *Proverbs 12:18*

Grasshoppers, because of their faithlessness, are envious of the faithful. Envy is a characteristic of the wicked. Envy is selfish ambition and greed, sprinkled with a reasonable portion of malice. It is no wonder that James attributes the cause of fights and quarrels among believers as being " . . . your desires that battle within you?" (4:1)

When people talk about you they are really frustrated with their own personal battle within. There is something about seeing someone else doing something correctly that infuriates those who do things incorrectly. Attitudely this translates into, "If I'm not doing it right, let's all do it wrong together."

Criticism for the sake of being critical is ungodly. Lies against truth are an abomination. To actively pursue a course of lies and deceit is deplorable. Ten spies saw the same thing, or did they? Eight saw the impossible because of their lack of faith. Two saw the probable and possible because of their ever increasing faith. The difference is the mentality of the viewer. Grasshoppers (some church folk) prefer the comfort of religiosity over the pursuit of victory. Can you imagine the scorn that Caleb and Joshua encountered over the next forty years? The faithless are compelled to attack the faithful for the sake of their own justification.

Chapter Four

TAKE YOUR MOUTH
OFF ME!

"Put them in mind to be subject to principalities and powers, to obey magistrates, to be ready to every good work, To speak evil of no man, to be no brawlers, but gentle, shewing all meekness unto all men. For we ourselves also were sometimes foolish, disobedient, deceived, serving divers lusts and pleasures, living in malice and envy, hateful, and hating one another. But after that the kindness and love of God our Saviour toward man appeared, Not by works of righteousness which we have done, but according to his mercy he saved us, by the washing of regeneration, and renewing of the Holy Ghost."

Titus 3: 1—5

The Apostle Paul is impressing upon Titus the importance of authority. He stresses "quietness and submission." Matthew

Henry comments, "We must not go up and down as tale-bearers, carrying ill-natured stories, to the prejudice of our neighbor's good name and the destruction of brotherly love. Misrepresentations, or insinuations of bad intentions, or of hypocrisy in what is done, things out of our reach or cognizance, these come within the reach of this prohibition. As this evil is too common, so it is of great malignity. [2]

Authority is to be respected, civil or spiritual. Loose uncharitable talk directed at authority is displeasing to God, and hurtful among men. Bad intentions and misguided speech represent disobedience before God.

> *"And he said unto his men, The LORD forbid that I should do this thing unto my master, the LORD'S anointed, to stretch forth mine hand against him, seeing he is the anointed of the LORD."*
>
> *1 Samuel 24:6*

> *"Saying, Touch not mine anointed, and do my prophets no harm."*
>
> *1 Chronicles 16:22*

Some thought must be given to what is said to, and about God's anointed. If the Lord Jesus Himself calls a person to ministry, He also anoints that person for the purpose of ministry. This means that God has His hands upon this mortal human. The question must be asked, "How much do you respect God's anointed and called?" It must be dangerous to offer malevolence towards a pastor or spiritual leader. It simply must be so! Regardless of personal opinion, God's Word is very clear. We know this is not to be stretched beyond the original intent of the Word. Men can challenge, discuss, even argue or debate with a pastor or spiritual leader. However, when it comes to misrepresentations, lies, harmful rumors, gossip, and even slander, dangerous ground has been reached.

> *"Fear ye not me? saith the LORD: will ye not tremble at my presence, which have placed the sand for the bound of the sea by a perpetual decree, that it cannot pass it: and though the waves thereof toss themselves, yet can they not prevail; though they roar, yet can they not pass over it? But this people hath a revolting and a rebellious heart; they are revolted and gone."*
>
> *Jeremiah 5:22,23*

Charles Spurgeon once wrote, "The majesty of God, as displayed in creation and providence, ought to stir up our hearts in adoring wonder and melt them down in willing obedience to his commands. The Almighty power of Jehovah, so clearly manifest in the works of his hands, should constrain us, his creatures, to fear his name and prostrate ourselves in humble reverence before his throne."[3]

Some people are so disobedient in their hearts, that only some supernatural calamity can make them obedient to God. We are a people poised for disaster because disaster is what we respond to. Prophetess Juanita Bynum, in her message delivered while preaching at Greater Imani Church & Christian Center says that God gives us "divine warnings." Jeremiah 11: 3–5 (ASV) states,

> *"And say to them, Thus says the LORD, the God of Israel, " Cursed is the man who does not heed the words of this covenant which I commanded your forefathers in the day that I brought them out of the land of Egypt, from the iron furnace, saying, ' Listen to My voice, and do according to all which I command you; so you shall be My people, and I will be your God,' in order to confirm the oath which I swore to your forefathers, to give them a land flowing with milk and honey, as {it is} this day. Then I said, " Amen, O LORD."*

The calling and anointing on God's leaders must be respected. I was in a Christian bookstore one day, and to my surprise, I could find only a few books on the subject of pastoral authority. Those that I found were ambiguous and apologetic. Church polity coupled with church political correctness, or the gross lack thereof, have forged the compromise of words regarding a spiritual leader's authority.

God calls us out of the muck and the mire. He lifts us out from ourselves to a place of heavenly usage. We are anointed and appointed to lead God's people, and that leadership should not be harnessed or bridled, especially by people placed in church authoritative roles and are not saved themselves. If we have the vision, then it is our duty to see that vision through to reality so that the people will not perish.

A close examination of great churches and ministries usually reveals strong leadership from the pulpit. God's anointed has the latitude to be the spiritual authority, and this authority precedes all others. This kind of leader delegates and appreciates the services of laity, but boldly confirms and maintains his or her commission and rank.

Verbal attacks and attempts of character assassination on God's leaders are reprehensible. I am well aware that there are those who purport to be in the service of the Lord but are not. There are those who abuse the authority and position that God gave them. Yes, there are despicable and unsavory types in pulpits, but there also are the "things of God." God, Himself, chooses to be the judge and jury in these matters, and often His judgment and punishment is revealed before man's very eyes.

Chapter Five
WHAT ARE YOU AFRAID OF? I AIN'T NEVER SCARED!

"And Saul said unto Samuel, I have sinned: for I have transgressed the commandment of the Lord, and thy words: because I feared the people, and obeyed their voice."

1 Samuel 15:24

Why should you be afraid of people talking about you? What you should fear is them not talking about you! The enemy verifies our anointing with his attacks. Without them we are not sure of our mission. Saul got caught up attempting to please the people at the expense of not pleasing God. He feared the people because of his personal insecurities and need for approval. You cannot pastor, lead, or guide the people of God according to their approval rating of you. Shepherds carry rods of authority to nudge, not beat the sheep in the direction they should go. Sheep would die of thirst and hunger without a Shepherd to lead and guide them.

If your ministry has become a "job" and your desire is to protect that "job" then you have vacated your rank and commission in the army of the Lord. You will be criticized and sometimes berated, but you may as well push ahead. Dr. Creflo Dollar wrote in his book "Uprooting The Spirit Of Fear," "He (Saul) fell into the trap of thinking that his position came from pleasing people rather than pleasing God. The result of this was in Saul losing everything: his kingship, his anointing, his calling, and finally his life."[4]

Religiosity causes people to forget the things of God. I continue to thank people for talking about me for "holy verification" alone. People that fear disapproval cannot be useful for the Kingdom.

Our anointing speaks simply of the Presence of God in our lives in a tangible way. Our experience of God tends to be progressive and so is what is called "the anointing."

"But my horn You have exalted like a wild ox; I have been anointed with fresh oil. My eye also has seen my desire on my enemies; my ears hear my desire on the wicked who rise up against me. The righteous shall flourish like a palm tree, He shall grow like a cedar in Lebanon. Those who are planted in the house of the LORD shall flourish in the courts of our God. They shall still bear fruit in old age; they shall be fresh and

flourishing, to declare that the LORD is right; He is my rock, and there is no unrighteousness in Him."

Psalms 92: 10—15 (NKJV)

With the anointing, we should see the desire of our enemies and our ears should hear the desire of the wicked who rise up against us. The Holy Spirit will show us that we will flourish regardless of what people say about us.

David received three anointings that would enable him to be a leader among God's people, and we need to study the manner in which he received them.

1. The anointing by Samuel.

"Now the LORD said to Samuel, "How long will you mourn for Saul, seeing I have rejected him from reigning over Israel? Fill your horn with oil, and go; I am sending you to Jesse the Bethlehem. For I have provided Myself a king among his sons."

1 Samuel 16:1 (NKJV)

"So he sent and brought him in. Now he was ruddy, with bright eyes, and good-looking. And the LORD said, "Arise, anoint him; for this is the one!" Then Samuel took the horn of oil and anointed him in the midst of his brothers; and the Spirit of the LORD came upon David from that day forward. So Samuel arose and went to Ramah."

1 Samuel 16: 12–13 (NKJV)

2. The anointing by Judah.

"Then the men of Judah came, and there they anointed David king over the house of Judah. And they told David, saying, "The men of Jabs Gilead were the ones who buried Saul."

2 Samuel 2:4 (NKJV)

3. The anointing by Israel.

"Therefore all the elders of Israel came to the king at Hebron, and King David made a covenant with them at Hebron before the LORD. And they anointed David king over Israel."

2 Samuel 5:3 (NKJV)

THE PLACE OF THE ANOINTING

"Now there was long war between the house of Saul and the house of David: but David waxed stronger and stronger, and the house of Saul waxed weaker and weaker. And unto David were sons born in Hebron: and his firstborn was Amnion, of Anhinga the Jezree-litess."

2 Samuel 3:1, 2

Hebron is entered by faith. It was the place Abraham dwelt after his separation from Lot.

WHAT ARE YOU AFRAID OF?
I AIN'T NEVER SCARED!

"Then Abram moved his tent, and went and dwelt by the terebinth trees of Mamre, which are in Hebron, and built an altar there to the LORD."

Genesis 13:18 (NKJV)

You see, Hebron is a place of communion. It is a place where God meets man at his place of need. Hebron is the place that we move to obediently. Hebron is the place where God separates us from the normal and mediocre. Hebron is the place of anointing.

To remain in Hebron takes faith. It was where Sarah was buried speaking of the resting place of faith.

"So Sarah died in Kirjath Arba (that is, Hebron) in the land of Canaan, and Abraham came to mourn for Sarah and to weep for her."

Genesis 23:2

Hebron is the place where promises are possessed. It is the place Joshua and Caleb saw, with the ten spies in Canaan, that Caleb later took for his own speaking of resting in possessions.

"And Joshua blessed him, and gave Hebron to Caleb the son of Jephunneh as an inheritance. Hebron therefore became the inheritance of Caleb the son of Jephunneh the Kenizzite to this day, because he wholly followed the LORD God of Israel. And the name of He-

41

bron formerly was Kirjath Arba (Arba was the greatest man among the Anakim). Then the land had rest from war."

Joshua 14:13–15 (NKJV)

Hebron results in fruitfulness and multiplication. It was a city where David had sons. Hebron brings the fullness of salvation. Hebron was a City of Refuge speaking of being free from judgment. It was a walled City, a place of protection. A place of Salvation was Hebron.

Hebron speaks of the communion that we have in Christ.

1. The first anointing frees us (to be who God wants us to be).
2. The second anointing fills us (with praise).
3. The third anointing fulfills us (to walk in the promised vision and inheritance).

"Those who are planted in the house of the LORD SHALL flourish in the courts of our God."

Psalm 92:13 (NKJV)

To flourish, God gives the "fresh oil anointing." Leaders in today's ministries and churches should pray for a "fresh oil anointing." The enemy is so busy attacking God's authority.

"But my horn You have exalted like a wild ox; I have been anointed with fresh oil."

Psalm 92:10 (NKJV)

Fresh means to be green, to be new, to be prosperous. Green is the color of resurrection life.

"Behold, thou art fair, my beloved, yea, pleasant: also our bed is green."

Song of Solomon 1:16

"He maketh me to lie down in green pastures: he leadeth me beside the still waters."

Psalm 23:2

There is something I want you to take notice of; David was "anointed" king over Israel. He wasn't just "chosen" but rather was anointed by God to be the leader of Israel at this historic time. David had received a "fresh oil anointing."

There is a difference between being chosen and being anointed. Chosen does not convert to success, but anointing does. Chosen does not convert to a victory, but anointing does. Yokes are destroyed because of the anointing, not because of being chosen. Men and women of God must seek after the anointing. It is not enough to just be called.

David was the anointed King of Israel. He was chosen by God, but walking in the realm of anointing and authority brings opposition. The anointing draws the ire of the enemy. The anointing in your own lives will usher in attacks by the enemy.

Some think of the anointing in terms of being seen and in the spotlight, but the anointing of God upon your life is a magnetic field for the enemy.

David was anointed by God as the King of Israel and all the news was not sitting well with the enemy. The reason for this is that David was not just anointed as king, but was also walking in the anointing!

When God conveys His anointing, we must not only enjoy the anointing, but we must walk in that anointing. In other words, the anointing is not given for the sake of fame, vanity or glory. It is given as an instrument of God for His work in the earth.

Being in the presence of the anointing doesn't make you anointed, just as being in McDonalds's doesn't make you a hamburger! Being in church doesn't make you anointed . . . only the touch of God upon your life makes you anointed as you walk in His ways!

Approval is a hard taskmaster. Seeking it from people is even harder. The attack of the enemy is to be expected and therefore not feared.

Chapter Six

THE ACCUSATIONS OF SATAN

"Then he showed me Joshua the high priest standing before the angel of the Lord, and Satan standing at his right hand to accuse him. The Lord said to Satan, "The Lord rebuke you, Satan! Indeed, the Lord who has chosen Jerusalem rebuke you. "Is this not brand plucked from the fire?" Now Joshua was clothed with filthy garments and standing before the angel."

Zechariah 3:1–3 (NASB)

The church does not have to listen to accusations by Satan and live in defeat. God revealed to Zechariah that the church is under attack by Satan. Joshua was the high priest standing before the angel of the Lord. Joshua was clothed in filthy garments, representing all of God's people.

In this heavenly courtroom scene, God the Father is the judge, Jesus the Advocate, is the defense attorney and the accused defendant is you (and me), represented by Joshua. His filthy garments represent our sin.

According to Judaic custom, when the high priest entered into the holy of holies, the place where the sacrifice of sin is offered, the priest had to make sure that he entered correctly and clean. If the priest was not perfect in his presentation, God might strike him dead on the spot. For this purpose the priests would have bells tied to the hems of their robes to signal movement, meaning they were still alive. Ropes would also be tied to their ankles so that their lifeless bodies could be pulled out in case of failure and death.

Satan looks at Joshua and says to God, "Look at him, he is filthy and full of sin." God declares that Satan has no authority to judge His people. This is the good news for us when we come up against accusations. Instead of the court of public opinion, God is our ultimate judge and Jesus is our Advocate.

Satan wants to point out our flaws, weaknesses, and guilt. He desires to destroy our usefulness. We have a lawyer that has never lost a case. We have an Advocate that has already paid our legal fees. Satan's accusations cannot stick because Jesus took our sins upon Himself on Calvary. We have been made right and correct before God. Just consider what happened in that courtroom.

> *"He spoke and said to those who were standing before him, saying, 'Remove the filthy garments from him.' Again he said to him, 'See, I have taken your iniquity away from you and will clothe you with festal robes.' Then I said, 'Let them put a clean turban on his head.'*

So they put a clean turban on his head and clothed him with garments, while the angel of the Lord was standing by."

Zechariah 3:4,5 (NASB)

Our correctness is holiness. We neither have to tie bells on our clothes, nor ropes around our ankles any longer. You cannot separate holiness from God, nor God from holiness. God is entirely beyond us; His thoughts are not our thoughts. His mind is not our mind. His ways are not our ways.

In the Old Testament, the high priest had to come into the presence of God with that rope tied around his ankle. If he was not practicing what he preached, living what he had taught, and believing what he said, the rope was needed to pull his limp body from the presence of God.

Jesus mediates our entrance into the presence of God. As God Himself, Jesus continues His second position of the triune God, just for our salvation. We share no common ground with God Almighty, but we do share common ground with His beloved Son. Jesus came out of the cosmos and took on flesh for the fitting and perfect sacrifice to end all sacrifices. Our holiness is projected through our love of Jesus. If we truly love Him we honor Him with our obedience.

We may have many accusers, but we need only one Advocate. Because God is holy, sin is a personal affront to His beauty, His holiness, and His character. Therefore we approach God with the cover of grace, shielding our sins from Him with the death and sacrifice of Jesus. No accuser can stand against Our Lord.

A believer must understand with clarity that a spiritual battle is being fought daily, but the good news is EVERY CHILD OF GOD HAS BEEN GIVEN A PROMISE OF VICTORY OVER SATAN! Consider the following scriptures:

Isaiah 54:17 "No weapon that is formed against thee shall prosper; and every tongue that shall rise against thee in judgment thou shalt condemn. This is the heritage of the servants of the Lord . . ."

Malachi 4:3 "And ye shall tread down the wicked; for they shall be ashes under the soles of your feet in the day that I shall do this, saith the Lord of hosts."

Luke 10:19 "Behold, I give unto you power to tread on serpents and scorpions, and over all the power of the enemy: and nothing shall by any means hurt you."

Romans 8:38–39 "For I am persuaded that neither death, nor life, nor angels, nor principalities, nor powers . . . nor height, nor depth, nor any other creature, shall be able to separate us from the love of God, which is in Christ Jesus our Lord."

James 4:7 " . . . Resist the devil, and he will flee from you."

1 John 4:4 "You . . . have overcome them: because greater is He that is in you, than he that is in the world."

Christians somehow forget that Adam turned the world over to the devil by his sin in the Garden of Eden and Satan, since that time, has been ruler of this world. John 12:31 states clearly, *"Now is the judgment of this world: now shall the prince of this world be cast out."* But God by His mercy and grace thwarted the enemy's attempt to take over completely. Man's restoration and redemption is promised just as it was in the Garden. God promised in Genesis 3:15 that His seed would come through the woman to crush Satan,

> *"And I will put enmity between thee and the woman, and between thy seed and her seed; it shall bruise thy head, and thou shalt bruise his heel."*

Meanwhile we are in a battle of spiritual warfare, and this is a battle that must be fought. You cannot sit on the fence or in the bleachers and watch as others fight. You must fight. We need to keep Satan from destroying our families, breaking up our marriages, owning our children, controlling our minds, and inflaming our passions. The authority for this kind of engagement is first found in the second chapter of Hebrews. The author of Hebrews says that God has another person in the spiritual battle, and he tells us that we need to see this person:

> *"We do see Him who has been made for a little while lower than the angels, namely, Jesus, because of the suffering of death crowned with glory and honor, that by the grace of God He might taste death for everyone"*
>
> *Hebrews 2:9 (NASB)*

If we are to be victors in this battle we must know Jesus, and understand this action on Calvary. In all actuality, Jesus has already won the battle for us. We just need to remind Satan every now and then. We must understand that the victory is really already won, but we must reinforce it from time to time against a persistent enemy that ignores the fact of his own defeat. Genesis 3:15 was the promise of Jesus. It was made good one night in a town called Bethlehem. Paul wrote in Galatians 4:4 (NASB), "When the fullness of the time came, God sent forth His Son, born of a woman, born under the Law."

Chapter Seven

FIGHTING LESSONS

"And when he had called unto him his twelve disciples, he gave them power against unclean spirits, to cast them out, and to heal all manner of sickness and all manner of disease"

Matthew 10:1

The Lord taught us in Luke 10:1–11,

> *"After these things the Lord appointed other seventy also, and sent them two and two before his face into every city and place, whither he himself would come. Therefore said he unto them, The harvest truly is great, but the labourers are few: pray ye therefore the Lord of the harvest, that he would send forth labourers into his harvest. Go your ways: behold, I send you forth as lambs among wolves. Carry neither purse, nor scrip, nor shoes: and salute no man by the way. And*

into whatsoever house ye enter, first say, Peace be to this house. And if the son of peace be there, your peace shall rest upon it: if not, it shall turn to you again. And in the same house remain, eating and drinking such things as they give: for the labourer is worthy of his hire. Go not from house to house. And into whatsoever city ye enter, and they receive you, eat such things as are set before you: And heal the sick that are therein, and say unto them, The kingdom of God is come nigh unto you. But into whatsoever city ye enter, and they receive you not, go your ways out into the streets of the same, and say, Even the very dust of your city, which cleaveth on us, we do wipe off against you: notwithstanding be ye sure of this, that the kingdom of God is come nigh unto you."

Then consider the results of Luke 10: 17–20,

And the seventy returned again with joy, saying, Lord, even the devils are subject unto us through thy name. And he said unto them, I beheld Satan as lightning fall from heaven. Behold, I give unto you power to tread on serpents and scorpions, and over all the power of the enemy: and nothing shall by any means hurt you. Notwithstanding in this rejoice not, that the spirits are subject unto you; but rather rejoice, because your names are written in heaven.

The key here is the knowledge of the Lord. Jesus

told the disciples do not rejoice because the spirits are subject to you, but rather to rejoice because your names are known in heaven. And if you are known in heaven, then your faith is known in hell. Remember Sceva and the other Jews who tried to cast out Satan in the name of Jesus, who Paul preached about. Satan replied in Acts 19:15 (NKJV), *"Jesus I know; and Paul I know; but who are you?"*

Some of us do not have the authority to cast out Satan because we don't know the Lord properly, and therefore are not feared by Satan. Then, there are some of us who cannot cast Satan out of anyone else because we are full of Satan ourselves. Jesus said in Mark 3:23, *"How can Satan cast out Satan?"* He said in Matthew 12:26, *"If Satan cast out Satan, he is divided against himself; how shall then his kingdom stand."* Then the Bible teaches us that a child cannot cast out their father. Jesus said in John 8:44, *"Ye are of your father the devil, and the lusts of your father ye will do."*

THE BODY OF CHRIST NEEDS A NEW FIGHTING SPIRIT

One of my ministers once said, "If you ask God for strength, He may just give you a problem." Problems are what we grow upon. Fighting the enemy is the spiritual aerobics of the soul. The enemy will talk about us, chastise us, abuse us, and falsely accuse us. But we are bigger than our enemies' feeble efforts to compromise our faith. I suggest that the Body of Christ needs a new "fighting spirit." For too long, we have sat idly by while Satan had his way.

The authority to fight the devil has been given to the church. The church is in a position of authority over Satan.

> *"And I say also unto thee, That thou art Peter, and upon this rock I will build my church; and the gates of hell shall not prevail against it"*

> *Matthew 16:18*

The same Peter that understood the truth of Jesus had previously been denounced by the Lord as having a mind on worldly things. Mark 8:31–38 gives us the story,

> *"And he began to teach them, that the Son of man must suffer many things, and be rejected of the elders, and of the chief priests, and scribes, and be killed, and after three days rise again. And he spake that saying openly. And Peter took him, and began to rebuke him. But when he had turned about and looked on his disciples, he rebuked Peter, saying, Get thee behind me, Satan: for thou savourest not the things that be of God, but the things that be of men. And when he had called the people unto him with his disciples also, he said unto them, Whosoever will come after me, let him deny himself, and take up his cross, and follow me. For whosoever will save his life shall lose it; but whosoever shall lose his life for my sake and the gospel's, the same shall save it. For what shall it profit a man, if he shall gain the whole world, and lose his own soul? Or what shall a man give in exchange for his soul? Whosoever*

therefore shall be ashamed of me and of my words in this adulterous and sinful generation; of him also shall the Son of man be ashamed, when he cometh in the glory of his Father with the holy angels."

Jesus rebuked the demon that spoke out of Peter. The believer has the authority, as a member of the body of Christ, to speak out and rebuke the demons that come and challenge us. The final decisive victory for defeating Satan was won at Calvary. The devil thought he had won but Jesus did not say, *"I am finished,"* He said *"It is finished!"*

Chapter Eight
THE TALK HURTS YOU BECAUSE YOU MAY BE SPIRITUALLY UNDEVELOPED!

"Therefore, laying aside falsehood, speak truth, each one of you, with his neighbor, for we are members of one another. Be angry, and yet do not sin; do not let the sun go down on your anger, and do not give the devil an opportunity"

Ephesians 4:25–27 (NASB)

Your emotions give Satan an entry into your lives. You must understand this relationship between your emotions and spiritual warfare. Failing to control anger, lusts, passion, emotions and desires offer the devil an opportunity to get a foothold in your life. Religious church people, the aforementioned "grasshoppers," that are not developed spiritually can only mouth the words of Jesus, and never have any results. They are like Sceva; imitating someone they knew who was close to the Lord. These people borrow the faith of others. You can be in church forever and never have any power. The church must be the means by which you develop as a Polaroid picture; slowly but surely, you develop from a blank page into a full image.

The spiritually developed are aware that a fight is going on and that their means of battle is spiritual. 2 Timothy 2:3–5 tells us:

"Thou therefore endure hardness, as a good soldier of Jesus Christ. No man that warreth entangleth himself with the affairs of this life; that he may please him who hath chosen him to be a soldier."

These spiritually developed individuals believe in suiting up for the battle.

"Put on the whole armor of God, that ye may be able to stand against the wiles of the devil, take unto you the whole armor of God, that ye may be able to withstand in the evil day, and having done all, to stand."

Ephesians 6:11,13

The spiritually "developed" understand whom they are fighting.

THE TALK HURTS BECAUSE YOU
MAYBE BE SPIRITUALLY UNDEVELOPED

"For we wrestle not against flesh and blood, but against principalities, against powers, against the rulers of the darkness of this world, against spiritual wickedness in high places"

Ephesians 6:12

Through Jesus Christ we have victory over Satan. Satan has no ability or authority other than what he has already displayed. He cannot come up with any new strategy or devices. It's the same old thing. Our job is to announce to the world who we are and whose we are. Satan has never been a match for God and Satan is no match for the spiritually developed.

The problem for most is weak faith. We are proclaimed free through Christ, but many have opted for captivity, bound by our lost hopes, failures, past sins and present pain.

I remember from Charles Schultz "Peanuts" Lucy says to Charlie Brown, "Charlie Brown, you are a foul ball in the line drive of life! You're often in the shadow of your own goal post! You're a miscue! You're three putts on the eighteenth green! You are a seven-ten split in the tenth frame! You have dropped a rod and reel in the lake of life! You're a missed free throw! You're a shanked nine-iron, a called third strike, a bug on the windshield of life; a roach walking into a roach motel!"[5]

The enemy will have you feeling like Charlie Brown, disabling your ability to overcome the world. Jesus gave His disciples both authority and power over demons. We have a right to rule over them.

Some of us have allowed the enemy to rob us of the completeness of our victory. We are raised by the action of Christ, but we are still walking around bound up in grave clothes like Lazarus.

> *"And when he thus had spoken, he cried with a loud voice, Lazarus come forth. And he that was dead came forth, bound hand and foot with grave clothes: and his face was bound about with a napkin. Jesus saith unto them, Loose him, and let him go."*
>
> *John 11:43,44*

Lazarus was able to come out of his grave, but he was not able to loosen his own grave clothes. Jesus ordered the disciples to loose him and let him go! His face was covered with a napkin, so even though he had come back to life he could not see the glory of his own deliverance. His napkin had to be removed by the disciples. This is the manner and commission of the church today. Many are living according to grace, but still are not delivered.

It is an awful thing to see living people wearing grave clothes. Yet, there are many, even in the church today, which have been made alive by the grace of Jesus Christ but they continue to wear their grave clothes.

Some are in such a state that, unless you asked them, you would think they were still dead. When Lazarus came forth perhaps someone said, "He must still be dead, he is wearing his grave clothes." To this Jesus would reply, "Loose him and let him go."

Chapter Nine

LEARNING TO BE COMFORTABLE IN A FIRE

"And the princes, governors, and captains, and the king's counselors, being gathered together, saw these men, upon whose bodies the fire had no power, nor was an hair of their head singed, neither were their coats changed, nor the smell of fire had passed on them."

Daniel 3:27

We need to revisit one of our favorite bible stories today, the miraculous account of three Hebrew boys, named Hananiah, Mishael, and Azariah. I would be as guilty as their oppressor if I denied them their real names first. You see Hananiah, Mishael, and Azariah will be renamed Shadrach, Meschach and Abednego by their Babylonian oppressors. Therefore, only for clarity, will I continue to refer to them as such.

For centuries, preachers have declared the glory of God

through the miraculous deliverance of these three boys from the fiery furnace. It is something to preach about. But the Lord opened my eyes and took me beyond the normal and apparent, and revealed to me through Revelation Knowledge that even if we are thrown into a fire, certain to perish, painful and brutal, we can become comfortable in that fire.

The heat that can come from unwarranted attacks by the enemy is sometimes unbearable. We want to surrender because the pressure is so great. But if we consider this scene in a Babylon furnace we can find comfort in fires.

The Apostle Paul wrote to Corinth,

"Are they Hebrews? so am I. Are they Israelites? so am I. Are they the seed of Abraham? so am I. Are they ministers of Christ? (I speak as a fool) I am more; in labors more abundant, in stripes above measure, in prisons more frequent, in deaths oft. Of the Jews five times received I forty stripes save one. Thrice was I beaten with rods, once was I stoned, thrice I suffered shipwreck, a night and a day I have been in the deep; In journeyings often, in perils of waters, in perils of robbers, in perils by mine own countrymen, in perils by the heathen, in perils in the city, in perils in the wilderness, in perils in the sea, in perils among false brethren; In weariness and painfulness, in watchings often, in hunger and thirst, in fastings often, in cold and nakedness. Beside those things that are without, that which cometh upon me daily, the care of all the churches. Who is weak,

and I am not weak? who is offended, and I burn not?
If I must needs glory, I will glory of the things which
concern mine infirmities."

2 Corinthians 11: 23–30

Paul says, "When it stormed on the sea, God sent an angel. When I was in the Philippian jail, God rocked the jail doors open and my shackles fell off. When I was trapped and about to be murdered, God let me down over the Macedonian wall. When I was stoned, God saved me. When a snake bit me, God removed the poison. On one occasion, one of my enemies trembled. On another occasion, an enemy said, "Almost thou persuadest me to be a Christian." When I went to God three times concerning the thorn in my flesh, God told me, "My grace is sufficient for thee." Paul is remembering Philippians 4:19,

"But my God shall supply all your need according to
his riches in glory by Christ Jesus."

Let's take a look at this scripture. "My God," deals with the exclusivity of His Being. "Shall supply," deals with the sovereignty of His Grace. "All your need," deals with His love and concern for you. "According to His riches in glory," is the power of the Holy Ghost. "By Christ Jesus," is the character of God's eternal Son.

Let's go further. "My God," tells us who He is. "Shall supply," explains His Infinite Resources. "All your need," is the Testimony of Faith. "According to his riches in glory," deals with the Promise of Faith. "By Christ Jesus," deals with the Hope of Faith.

Let's go deeper. "My God to His riches in glory," is the object. Let's go even deeper, "My God," is the source of the supply. "Shall," is the certainty of the supply. "Supply," is the fullness of the supply. "All you need," is the extent of the supply. "According to His riches," is the measure of the supply. "In glory," is the storehouse of the supply. "By Christ Jesus," is the channel of your supply.

Paul says, "I will glory in the things of which I have suffered." If we are to be faithful believers, we must understand that there is always a purpose to our suffering. God reveals his glory in us. There is a purpose in your suffering. There is an opportunity in your suffering. God did not bring you this far just to leave you.

Shadrach, Meschach, and Abednego were placed in the fiery furnace because of their refusal to stop praying to their God, and pray to the god of Nebuchadneezer.

We need to look at prayer as taking hold of God's eagerness, not overcoming God's reluctance. Let us research the scriptures:

Jeremiah 33:3 says, *"Call to Me, and I will answer you, and I will tell you great and mighty things, which you do not know."*

John 14:13,14 states,

"And whatever you ask in My name, that will I do, that the Father may be glorified in the Son. If you ask Me anything in My name, I will do it."

You know that the Lord will get into your fire with you

and make you become comfortable. Nebuchadneezer saw four men in that fire. Jesus made a pre-incarnate appearance in the Old Testament just to get in the fire with Shadrach, Meschach, and Abednego. He could not wait for Bethlehem when He saw the faithfulness of these three Hebrews.

He leaped out of heaven and into that fiery furnace. The fire was too hot for those who threw the three into the fire; they perished. You need to understand today that when you find yourself in a fire, just be comfortable, the Lord is with you.

However, I need to go further and tell you that something did burn in that fiery furnace. Maybe we don't focus on it as we should, but I want to tell you that something did burn that day in that furnace, and I'm not talking about those soldiers that threw them in. Daniel 3:21 states,

"Then these men were bound in their coats, their hosen, and their hats, and their other garments, and were cast into the midst of the burning fiery furnace."

The only thing that burned in that furnace was the rope that bound them. The ropes burned. What had them bound released them.

If you will trust the Lord and be comfortable in your situation; be comfortable in your circumstance; comfortable in your dilemma; comfortable in your bad finances; comfortable in your illness; comfortable in your broken marriage; be comfortable in your shaky job; comfortable in broken relationships, and be comfortable when people verbally attack you, God will remove those things that bind you.

"And God is able to make all grace abound toward you; that ye, always having all sufficiency in all things, may abound to every good work. "

2 Corinthians 9:8

Chapter Ten

SIZE DOES NOT MATTER!

"We are troubled on every side, yet not distressed; we are perplexed, but not in despair; persecuted, but not forsaken; cast down, but not destroyed; always bearing about in the body the dying of the Lord Jesus . . ."

2 Corinthians 4: 8–10

There are times in our lives when we major in minor things and minor in major things. We go through the struggles of life, endlessly searching for peace. One problem may often lead to another. A good day, most often, will be followed by a bad one. Sometimes problems seem to never cease. But as we live on, we grow to realize that those problems were not so big after all.

It's not the boulders we stumble over, it's the pebbles. It's not the logs that trip us up, it's the twigs. It's not the eagles that worry us, it's the mosquitoes. Frustrations come from the inability to control our lives. The Apostle Paul understood frustrations well. For most of his life he was frustrated with pain. He called his pain a thorn in his flesh.

2 Corinthians 12: 7–9 states,

"And lest I be exalted above measure through the abundance of the revelations, there was given to me a thorn in the flesh, the messenger of Satan to buffet me, lest I should be exalted above measure. For this thing I besought the Lord thrice, that it might depart from me. And He said unto me, My grace is sufficient for thee: for my strength is made perfect in weakness."

Paul's thorn was his frustration. Frustrated that there was something in his life that he had no control over. He sought the Lord three times about the matter but the Lord replied to him that,

"My grace is sufficient for thee: for my strength is made perfect in weakness."

God chose not to remove Paul's frustration because it was his frustration that kept him in check. Some of us need to be kept in check. Some people consider roses beautiful. But I would like to suggest, it's the thorns that make them beautiful. Amidst the thorns the beauty of the rose is displayed. In God's manner of blessing thorns, frustration, and pain become a means of going from frustration to revelation.

You see, with thorns our vision is sharpened, that we may see what God has wanted us to see. With thorns, we begin to hear the things we failed to hear before. With thorns we begin to sensitize our feelings, that we may feel what we have failed to feel before. With a little pain and frustration of our own, we increase our compassion, that we may love someone we have failed to love before. With just a little discomfort, we enlarge our understanding, that we may comprehend that which we have failed to comprehend before.

The enemy wants our frustrations to lead us to breakdowns, depression and destruction, but God uses them to develop us.

I've placed many thoughts in this book regarding verbal attacks of the enemy. I am thankful for every bad thing ever said about me. I have withstood the best that Satan could offer.

There are so many ministers and ministries in harms way. Jealously within the body is sometimes horrific. Frustrations run high among those that desired so much in ministry but have realized so little. Envy overcomes the faithful as they ponder why he is succeeding and I am failing.

The truth is that there is always victory in every cause for Christ. The size of a ministry and number of members is not always the indicator of successful ministry. Your anointing may be for a select few, while mine may be for an unknown many. God's purpose can be reached by small congregations as well as large ones. Envy will remove an anointing and disable a ministry.

There is always someone that is bigger, a congregation that is larger, a ministry that is more visible and a minister that is more popular.

I applaud and thank God for every ministry that is holding up the "blood stained banner." Not only that, but I delight in their successes. I revel in their accomplishments. I shout and praise God for their numbers.

The threat facing the body of Christ today comes from within. Satan has developed a sophisticated plan to pit us against each other, utilizing our emotions as the weapons.

Sometimes traditional churches and ministries cannot realize possession because they are frozen on promise. There is a time when God challenges us to get up off our knees and claim our inheritance. God has to lift up another generation that is not caught up in the pain of the past; a generation that is not fixated on the failures of yesterday, but excited about the possibilities of tomorrow. Bitterness has a way of infecting the future. A bitter heart curtails the possibility of tomorrow.

There is a "new move" of God in the earth. Instead of being led by a pillar of smoke and fire, we are now to be led by the Holy Spirit. God's Spirit takes us from promise to possession. . .

Romans 8:16,17 tells us,

"The Spirit itself beareth witness with our spirit, that we are the children of God, and if children, then heirs; heirs of God and joint heirs with Christ; if so be that we suffer with him, that we may be also glorified together."

Paul writes in Philippians 4:6,

"Be careful for nothing."

Don't worry about what people say.

Don't worry about what people think.

Don't worry about what people do.

Don't worry about how they perceive you.

Paul continues in that sixth verse,

"But in everything by prayer and supplication with thanksgiving let your requests be made known unto God."

Your enemy cannot understand how you can have peace in the midst of their attack on you. The devil is bewildered by those that can find peace in the midst of a storm. God's peace passeth all understanding.

There may be times when you think you are going to lose your mind. There are times when you think you cannot take anymore. But if you keep on working, the Lord's promise is that He shall keep your hearts and minds through it all.

Your success is dependent on the nature of your mind. Paul writes,

"Finally, brethren, whatsoever things are true, whatsoever things are honest, whatsoever things are just, whatsoever things are pure, whatsoever things are lovely, whatsoever things are of good report; if there be any virtue, and if there be any praise, think on these things."

Philippians 4:8

ABOUT THE AUTHOR

Bill Adkins is anointed of God to impart and activate the gifts of the Spirit in order to raise up strong ministries in the Body of Christ. This gifted visionary with a true apostolic and prophetic call on his life, has a desire to infiltrate the world with the Word of God. He is dedicated to perfecting the saints and training ministers to fulfill the call of God in their lives. Through his transition from pastoral to the apostolic, he is bridging the gap between denominations regarding living in the Spirit and gifts of the Spirit. He accepts his charge to raise up a fresh new movement of holiness, parenting as a spiritual father, traditional churches and denominations into the beauty of holiness.

He and his lovely wife Linda also own and operate Adkins and Associates, a public relations consulting firm. Apostle Adkins is the father of four children, Taihia, Ronne,' Christopher and William, III.

Active and alert to the needs of people, Apostle Bill Adkins has stood before mayors, governors, presidents and international dignitaries on behalf of causes and concerns. He is recognized around the world as a humanitarian and scholar. He serves as the Chief Apostle, Senior Pastor and Founder of the 6,000 member-plus Greater Imani Church and Christian Center and the Imani Telecast Network, USA, headquartered in Memphis.

Bill Adkins has led numerous missionary journeys to Africa and the Caribbean, establishing health clinics in Koalack Senegal, Banjul, Gambia and Kumasi, Ghana. He has actively supported numerous economic development efforts on the African continent by serving as a member of the Constituency for Africa (CFA), a Washington, DC based lobbying organization. Dr. Adkins spoke extensively throughout South Africa on the virtues of free elections and served as an observer for the Republic of South Africa's first open election.

On the home front, this visionary leader founded Greater Imani Church and Christian Center on November 1, 1989 with 29 dedicated friends and family members. Since that time Greater Imani has enjoyed phenomenal growth, making it what some have called, "The Fastest Growing Church in America." Greater Imani also enjoys the reputation of "the" church with the largest male population and percentage in America. Dr. Kwanza Kunjufu wrote, "Greater Imani breaks the mold of the stereotypical female dominated black church. On my speaking engagement there, I noticed there were more men than women in attendance."

Dr. Adkins received the distinction of being one of the few Americans enstooled as an Ashanti Chief in Ghana and given the title and name Nana Osei Tutu which is the name of the current Asantehene (King of the Ashanti's). His ministry reaches thousands of households via his weekly television program, Up My People. He is the author of FROM AFRICA TO BETHLEHEM, MY HOUSE/GOD'S HOUSE, DRY GROUND THEOLOGY and most recently, LIVING IN THE SPIRIT.

NOTES

1. Larry Crabb, <u>Soul Talk: Speaking with Power Into the Lives of Others</u> (Integrity Publishers, 2003) p.76

2. Matthew Henry, <u>Complete Commentary on the Whole Bible</u> (Hendrickson Publishers, 1991) Titus 3

3. Charles H. Spurgeon, <u>The Treasury of the Bible</u>, vol. 4 (Grand Rapids, MI: Zondervan Publishing House, 1962) p.18

4. Dr. Creflo A. Dollar, Jr. Uprooting the Spirit of Fear (Harrison House Publishers, 2002)

5. Charles Schultz, <u>You've Had It, Charlie Brown</u> ("Peanuts," 1969)

Contact Bill Adkins
P.O. Box 280199
Memphis, TN 38168
Call Toll Free: 1–877–274–6264
Visit us on the web at:
www.billadkinsministries.com

or order more copies of this book at

TATE PUBLISHING, LLC

127 East Trade Center Terrace
Mustang, Oklahoma 73064

(888) 361 - 9473

Tate Publishing, LLC

www.tatepublishing.com